We

Sarah Freligh

Harbor Editions
Small Harbor Publishing

Cover art and design by Luke Blevins
Book layout by Allison Blevins

WE
SARAH FRELIGH
ISBN 978-1-7359090-0-4
Harbor Editions,
an imprint of Small Harbor Publishing

All the girls, everywhere

CONTENTS

We

ANN ARBOR, 1974

Sky bruising purple when I stuck out
my thumb and caught a fast ride
west in a spoke-wheeled Cadillac
with three geezers who passed

a silver flask of Scotch, honeyed
with age, and even I sang along
with Sinatra on the car stereo, soprano
blanketing their reedy tenors, all the way

to South Bend where the driver
handed me a Hershey bar and a wad
of ones. I played pinball for hours
at the Greyhound station, high

on horsepower and whiskey,
an eternity before the bus
chuffed in. How is it that time
is slow and heavy as an elephant

when you're young and impatient to get
to the next second? Now, the merry-
go-round of years, a heartbeat
between Christmases. It's like you

go out a girl who can honky tonk
all night and come home old, smelling
of spiced apples and cat, fat
with memories coding your bones.

EPIDEMIC

Because Davie Gray is protected by the blood of Jesus and his scripture-spouting pastor daddy, he stays in the classroom practicing his times tables while the rest of the class waits outside the gymnasium, sleeves rolled, for the stern-faced nurses to swab and stab us with the biggest needles in the history of the world, according to Markie Wolf, who will faint at the very sight of it, or Judd French who Darlene Meadows will tell us *cried like a little baby* though he looked just fine by the time we break into groups of three and argue over what color to make the map of the Dakotas, *green or blue* I say though Judd insists on brown because of the Badlands while Davie just sits there coloring and quiet.

Because we are inoculated, none of us will get the mumps that year or the next, though Davie Gray will spend a month in the hospital in eighth grade and come back to us a shadow, skinny as a scarecrow and sterile, according to Darlene who claimed she overheard her nurse mother say the sickness settled in his balls and turned him sterile as a donkey, which is how the joke got started *How is a starter's pistol like Davie Gray?*, answer, *Both of them shoot blanks,* something we will ha-ha over until the day Davie shows up at school with his father's gun in his black backpack and shoots his way through the cafeteria before the cops show up and lead him away but not before he kills six people, Judd and some other jocks and a lunch lady, and for weeks the school will be lit up with television cameras and microphones tethered to women with glossed-on faces who talk about *never forgetting* what happened here but there will be a mall the next week and after that a synagogue and a movie theater and a mall again until we lose track, an *epidemic of violence* say the glossed-on faces before tossing to the weather guy for tomorrow's forecast *more rain on the way.* And sometimes I think about hunting down Davie Gray, but I never do, though what I did do once was drive through North Dakota where I took a cell phone shot at sunset of the Badlands, which weren't bad at all, in fact they were kind of lovely in their shadowed dark.

THOSE GIRLS

Olga was fast as a muscle car, one of those girls. There on Friday, gone by Monday to care for a sick aunt in Florida. We knew better. We knew she'd be back in nine months, flattened, her brass tarnished. Smudged with the fingerprints of all who had driven her.

WE DIVE

Age 12, we dive and dive. For the girl playing dead by the drain in the deep end of the pool. For the pennies we toss in the water by the lifeguard's chair. From the diving board—three steps, the hurdle, the launch. We come up for air long enough to eat lunch, cheeseburgers and fries drowned in a murder of ketchup. Our bellies, humped and rounded, push against the elastic of our bathing suits as we dive and dive and dive.

At 14, we lie in the gutters of the swimming pool, basting our bellies in baby oil and the occasional wavelets of cool that slop up whenever a boy dives in. We pick at burgers without buns, drink cans of Tab poured warm over ice that cracks like knuckles. We learn about calories and fat from the high school girls who shout warnings across the humid locker room. Sometimes we dive but only at the end of the day.

At 18, we arrange chaise lounges and serve up the buffet of ourselves, tasty swell of breasts toasted brown, a feast for our boyfriends teeing off on the first hole. Later we pull out hand mirrors and paint alien faces over our eyes and lips, wait by the 18th green while they putt out. We prop our feet on the dashboard of their cars, let them drive us to a rutted field off a dirt road where we unzip them and dive as if we are starving. We hold our breath, but we've already smothered. Already drowned.

ANY BODY

Down under was your stomach, hollowed out and shouting. What it said, you didn't listen. You counted ribs, a xylophone of bones that lullabied you into sleep.

You heard *beautiful*. From the six-ounce glass of tomato juice that stunned your tongue. From the fork you stabbed into lettuce leaves, in the cube of cheddar cheese that fueled your six-mile run along country roads. Whole rows of corn bowed down and whispered: *Beautiful*. The east-west swish of cars on Interstate 70, *beautiful, beautiful, beautiful*.

Your world simpled into an equation of *yes* or *no*. No to the smear of chocolate frosting on cellophane, to chicken thighs frying, to glistening coins of pepperoni on a discarded slice. A storm of *no,* so much thunder and lightning. But *yes* to your hipbones sharpening the pockets of your size five Levis, to the bathroom tiles cool white against your cheek. *Yes* to water when you withered and curled.

Nights you bloomed under black lights, danced with your dwindling shadow. When the fat lady cut in, you knew to excuse yourself before she could crawl inside to live in you. In the bathroom, you leaned against the sink and whispered *yes*. Afterward, you were clean again. Hollowed out and shouting.

MAKEUP

The hoodie girl in your homeroom, the fat one who carries condoms in her purse, says to ditch the pink lipstick. Eyeliner, a gob of mascara, what it will take to saddle up and ride with her and her friends who herd by the window in the third floor girls' room, lit cigarettes in hand. You yearn to smoke elegant like your mother, deliberate, the punctuation she inserts before exhaling and saying *No*. Because you ache to break from the corral of country club boys and their callused golf hands, you skip fifth hour and let that hoodie girl sit you down on a toilet seat and paint you up into somebody else. Somebody who'd look good riding shotgun, bourbon-breathed, arm cocked on an open window. Someone at home with a cigarette in her hand exhaling *yes, yes, yes*.

BABIES, BECAUSE

We had them because the rubber broke while hot and heavy in the backseat of the drive-in, because ginger-ale was an old wives tale. We had them because there was no morning-after pill, not yet, no abortion that wasn't back-alley Detroit or two weeks in Sweden. Because nice girls refused to tuck rubbers in the coin purse of their billfolds. Because we were okay with the whispers —in the aisles of the A&P or later at graduation when we crossed the stage with a belly out to here. Because we were mostly okay with all of it until the afternoon of the baby shower when we passed joints and a warm bottle of Andre and cried a little about all the life we'd never get to live because, face it, we were the girls who had to have them.

GOOD GIRLS

Summer a long time ago, before everything changed, when all we did all day was show up at the pool and claim the corner farthest from the lifeguard and the bratty kids so we could pass around the thermos of margaritas heavy on the tequila that Penny filched from her father and when we got too high or too hot, we'd wade into the pool until we were turquoise with water and stay there until we were cool again and only then would we walk back up the stairs, slowly so all the boys could see the little slices of us, give them a taste of what we might be in a dark car before we yanked down our bikini bottoms and became good girls again.

LIGHT YEARS

Tonight the moon's an orange wedge, frazzle-
edged leftover stuck to a gray bowl of twilight

sky, orange like the bartender used to slice
in the slow hour before five o'clock rush,

tossed into the garnish trough for us
waitresses to thread onto swizzle sticks

I'd balance across the lip
of a drink, a Collins or a whiskey sour—

Lady Drinks, I thought of them, drunk
by women with diamonds the size of gumballs

weighing heavy on ring fingers. The husband
ordered. Always. *She'll have*, he'd say, and leer

at me, his co-conspirator, while she stared
out at the putting green where college

guys, adorable in shorts, competed for beer.
An orange slice or two was all I ate

some nights. I'd stuff down my hunger
with water and a quick cigarette out back

on the freight dock where dishwashers
passed a joint and named

the constellations for me: the Big Dipper, Orion
and his flashy Elvis belt of stars; Cassiopeia,

wife of Cepheus, sentenced to life
in the sky for boasting she

was more beautiful than the sea
nymphs, comely and younger. At night's end

I unfurled white linens fresh
from plastic bags, set my tables

with silver still hot to the touch
Only then could I punch out, spill

into the night, headlong toward
the next minute when something

or anything could happen.
The earth was turning, tilting

fat on its axis and I ached
for a kingdom to be queen of.

A KIND OF MAGIC

He tells me that his mother carries a lock of his dead father's hair coiled inside the folded bills of her wallet, how she'll forget about it altogether and have to pluck it, embarrassed, from the spill of dimes and nickels on the check-out counter at the grocery store. Sometimes she'll tell the startled cashier that it's *her* hair from when she was a natural blonde, when her hair hung thick and straight to the ass of her tie-dyed mini-skirt, when she went by the name of Star Aster and danced naked in the rain at Woodstock. Way before she was somebody's mother or the widow of a man who left her with nothing but a shoebox full of unpaid bills and three photographs from their honeymoon in Vegas, their faces smudged gray with fatigue after a night at the craps table where they wagered everything but their round-trip Greyhound tickets from Ann Arbor. Back when his blond hair hid his eyes, curtained his face as he kissed the dice. Back when she would bet anything was possible, when she still believed love was a kind of magic.

GODDESSES

The year I dropped out of college,
I didn't know what I wanted
from life and declaring a major
seemed too much like a groove
I'd fit my wheels in and travel on
until I was sixty-five, happy
or not. But I was tired of being
broke, tired of smoke and endless
ass pats from drunks at the bar
where I schlepped pitchers of cold
Bud and tequila shots for dime
tips. At Playgirl Figure Salon I'd cater
to women who wouldn't touch me,
despite the fact that I looked pretty
good in the black and white leotard V-ing
to cleavage, the stretchy fabric that reined
in the beer gut I'd grown. I was eager
to breathe fresh air, to lead a class in jumping
jacks and torso twists designed to slim
the midriff, show ladies how to properly
heft a five-pound barbell that would rid
their triceps of the flab they hid
in sleeved shirts. But, no, my job
was to con them into signing up
by sharing photos of women none
of us knew, before and after shots, claim
we'd made them this way, like goddesses
waving our skinny wands. I sold
a six-month membership to a woman
with shadowed eyes who smelled
of cigarettes and beer at nine in the morning.
Her hand shook: *I want my husband*

not to recognize me, she said. I called in sick
the next day and the day after, claiming
my mother's cancer had metastasized
and I was needed at home. I lied.
My mother died years later of cancer,
almost as if I'd predicted it, made it
so, but no, you can go crazy
that way, believing you are goddess
enough to make shit happen.

AWAY

We spent our last three bucks on a tallboy that we passed back and forth through most of Iowa. Twenty-four hours we'd been driving, away from the city and the sirens and the stink of the streets. Truckers honked around us, past us. We waved to the cute ones, hiked our skirts higher on our pale thighs. We were down to warm suds when the needle scraped "E" and we pulled into a Mom and Pop station at the next exit. We sat on the curb out front and discussed what we were willing to do for a gallon or two—steal? sell ourselves?—and laughed until our pants were damp. The owner called us *Sweethearts* and gave us coffee and a couple of stale doughnuts before he shut off the lights and headed home. I'd never seen so many stars. Sitting there like that, I was sure I could feel the earth turn but you said no, it was only the grumble of trucks on the interstate. Still it was nice to think we were moving forward, away from ourselves, even while we were stuck.

WHAT I LIKED BEST

was punching out, the satisfying chunk of time
stamp on card signaling that work day
was history. Especially in the afternoon.
Especially in August when I wore the grease
and heat of lunch rush like a uniform
I'd worked hard for and earned. Maybe
I changed in the ladies room. Maybe
I merely shucked my white apron, traded
my stained waitress shoes for sandals
and headed for the bar down the road
that was dark and cool as a cave. We
threw down our waitress money, blizzards
of bills we pulled from pockets and purses, sure
there would always be more, paid for
drinks and paper cradles of fries so hot
from the fryer they sizzled
a blister on the front of my tongue. And what I liked
best was when the afternoon turned the corner
toward evening and the mothers among us
drifted off to fix dinner for kids or husbands
leaving us singles to order another round
we maybe chased with a shot, enough
reason to turn toward each other and show
off the selves we hid each day under our uniforms,
the girls who said sir and ma'am and thank you
for nothing. In the bar, we could dream
big, cop to it without apology, and when we sailed out
into the dusk, first stars hatching in a vast
indigo nest of sky, we wished on the first
one whose pulse and glitter caught
our eye, full up enough to believe
we'd someday get what we asked for.

LAST CHRISTMAS

We talked often about what to give someone who was dying: *Nothing. Everything. A little something.* My sister and I went to Walmart on a Sunday in December. It was crowded: Spit-polished people wearing church clothes, frat guys in pajama pants swigging Red Bulls. Everyone wandering aimless through the aisles, faces bathed sick by yellow fluorescence. Speakers bleated out Christmas music interrupted by announcements for lost kids. When we got lost in electronics, in the middle of a football game, a dozen running backs came for us. We found a set of dishes, white and light and dishwashable, *something Dad could handle.* A mom smacked her kid for yanking down a stack of blankets. The air smelled of something sweet and on fire. Outside a man shook a bell over a red kettle. The snow had picked up, filling in footprints. We had to blaze our own trail.

LETTER TO A FRIEND IN MAY

Late April when the snow finally melted, not
in a flood but a gradual retreat, a letting go

revealing the hurt earth underneath, the mud
and the hostas, fragile shoots for now. Finally

warm enough today to transplant the seedlings,
nasturtiums and zinnias, give them a taste

of what life will be like outside. Hands in
the dirt, I thought of your brother and mine

and how in the midst of all these beginnings, someone
somewhere is always ending. The cycle

of life, mesh of gears and speed, grinding
on. I know time heals what wounds us, but try

to tell me in January that winter will end.
That under a foot of snow a seed can grow.

WHAT WE REMEMBER

The holy roller girl who writhed with the fever of Jesus on Sunday while her pastor daddy twirled snakes like lariats over the heads of sinners crying to be cleansed. Who bused in from out-county on Monday, undressed for gym in a mop closet. Who stuffed a transistor radio down her pants while her pastor daddy handed out salvation in front of Sears. Who believed she'd ascended to heaven whenever Diana Ross sang in her ears, all gauze and sequins, whenever Smoky *baby baby*-ed her down rows of corn where she danced with her tall green partners. The nights her father came to sanctify her. The day she collapsed in gym class and sang to Jesus in her gospel tongue, an arpeggio of gibberish, all amen and hell yes. How she came back to us a ghost girl, rinsed of all but the hard, high notes.

ACKNOWLEDGMENTS

Grateful acknowledgment is made to the editors of the following journals in which these works, or earlier versions of them, first appeared:

50-Word Stories: "Those Girls"

Cease, Cows: "We Dive"

Cincinnati Review: "Any Body"

Diode: "Ann Arbor, 1974" and "Letter to a Friend in
       May"

Eleven Eleven: "Goddesses"

Emerge: "Good Girls"

Fractured Lit: "Epidemic"

Hotel Amerika: "Light Years"

Jellyfish Review: "Last Christmas"

Milk Candy Review: "What We Remember"

Spelk: "Babies, Because"

Typehouse: "What I Liked Best"

Vestal Review: "A Kind of Magic"

Wigleaf: "Away"

Sarah Freligh is the author of *Sad Math*, winner of the 2014 Moon City Press Poetry Prize and the 2015 Whirling Prize from the University of Indianapolis; *A Brief Natural History of an American Girl* (Accents Publishing, 2012); and *Sort of Gone* (Turning Point Books, 2008). Recent work has been featured on Writer's Almanac, appeared in the *Cincinnati Review*, *SmokeLong Quarterly*, *Diode*, and in the anthologies *New Micro: Exceptionally Short Fiction* (Norton 2018) and *Best Microfiction* 2019 and 2020. Among her awards are a 2009 poetry fellowship from the National Endowment for the Arts and a grant from the Constance Saltonstall Foundation in 2006. She lives and swims in Rochester, New York.

.

Made in United States
North Haven, CT
20 August 2022

22930181R00019